Feeling Good On The Inside

(Feeling Good To Be Alive)

You Always Have Other Options

Which one will you choose?

Written by
Janine Fletcher

Book illustrations by

_____

(Write your own name here)

Where you see a picture frame, draw a picture about what you've just read.

DISCLAIMER

The suggestions in this book for personal growth are not meant to substitute for the advice of a trained professional such as a medical doctor, psychologist, therapist etc. It is essential to consult such a professional in the case of any physical or mental symptoms.

Feeling Good On The Inside

YAHOO Feel Good Series

Being Your Own Best Friend
(Feeling Good To Be Me)

Feeling Good On The Inside
(Feeling Good To Be Alive)

What A Wonderful World
(Feeling Good To Live In This World)

Meet Owen ...

Draw Owen here

The first thing you probably notice about Owen is that he looks happy.
His eyes are sparkling, he has a smile on his face, he's standing up straight
and there's a kind of glow about him.

Meet Jack...

```
┌─────────────────────────────────────┐
│ Draw Jack here                       │
│                                      │
│                                      │
│                                      │
│                                      │
│                                      │
│                                      │
│                                      │
│                                      │
│                                      │
│                                      │
│                                      │
│                                      │
└─────────────────────────────────────┘
```

The first thing you probably notice about Jack is that he looks sad and angry. You can't really see his eyes properly because his head is hanging down and he's looking at the ground, but there is no sparkle in his eyes. He has a frown on his face, his body is slumped over and there's a kind of dullness about him.

That's what Owen and Jack look like on the outside.

I wonder what they feel like on the inside.

Let's look inside Owen first.

Owen feels happy and relaxed.
His stomach feels calm.
His heart feels open.
His breathing is soft, deep and easy.
He feels comfortable in his own skin.
Inside Owen feels good.

Now, let's look inside Jack.

Jack feels angry and sad.
He has a sinking feeling in his stomach.
His heart feels closed.
It is hard for him to breathe.
He feels uncomfortable in his own skin.
Inside Jack doesn't feel good.

Draw Owen here

Draw Jack here

I wonder why Owen and Jack are so different.

Jack wondered about this too.

Owen and Jack went to the same school; they were even in the same grade.

They both lived in the same street and they often raced their bikes on the track in the park at the end of their street.

They played in the same basketball team and they had swimming lessons together.

They were both good at math, but needed help with their reading.

They did so many things the same - except Owen felt good and Jack didn't. Day after day, it was the same. No matter what happened, Owen would end up feeling good and Jack would end up feeling bad.

Jack just couldn't understand it. It didn't seem fair. Jack thought that there must be some secret that Owen had. So, he decided to become a detective, watch everything that Owen did, and see if he could discover Owen's secret. Then maybe he would start to feel good too

When they lost a game of basketball this is what happened …

Jack ignored the other team, walked off sulking, mumbling to himself, "It was the umpires' fault! We should have won."
Jack didn't feel good.

Then he remembered to watch what Owen did.

Owen shook the hands of all the players from the other team and said, "Congratulations, great game."
"Thanks, you played a great game too", the other team said to Owen.
Even though his team lost, he had enjoyed the game.
Owen felt good.

Draw Jack here	Draw Owen here

They had their swimming lesson, the instructor asked each of them to swim a lap. When he told them both how they could improve, this is what happened…

The instructor told Jack that if he slowed his arms down a bit and cupped his hands more he would be able to swim faster.

"It's not fair", Jack thought to himself "I never do anything right. He's always picking on me!"

Jack didn't take any notice of what the instructor said, and he didn't swim any faster.

Jack didn't feel good.

Then he remembered to watch what Owen did.

The instructor told Owen that if he slowed his arms down a bit and cupped his hands more he would be able to swim faster. Owen did exactly what the instructor told him and he did swim faster than he ever had.

"Wow! That was amazing!" Owen said to the instructor, "Thanks for your help."

Owen had improved his swimming technique and he was grateful for the instructor's help.

Owen felt good.

Where you see a picture frame, draw a picture about what you've just read.

Draw Jack at his swimming lesson

Draw Owen at his swimming lesson

They had a special class to help with their reading and when the teacher asked them to have a go and see if they could do the activity on their own first, this is what happened...

Jack didn't understand what he was meant to do and he thought to himself, "I'm so dumb, I hate reading anyway."
He just sat there and didn't do anything.
Jack didn't feel good.

Then he remembered to watch what Owen did.

Owen didn't understand what he was meant to do either so he asked the teacher to explain it to him. The teacher showed Owen how to do the work and then Owen understood.
"Thanks for your help", Owen said to the teacher "I understand now."
Now he knew what to do, the work was easy for him.
Owen kept working until he had finished and any time he wasn't sure what to do, he just asked the teacher to explain it to him.
He was learning a lot and his reading was getting better all the time.
Owen felt good.

Draw Jack at his reading class

Draw Owen at his reading class

When it was time for math class, the teacher said that the class wouldn't be able to play a game until everyone had finished their work.

Math was both Owen's and Jack's favourite subject at school.

They were the first two to finish and this is what happened...

Jack looked at Sam's work and saw that he hadn't even started.

He thought to himself,

"This is so boring having to wait for dumb Sam to finish his work.

We'll never get to have a game and it's all his fault."

Jack was feeling really bored and he didn't feel good.

Then he remembered to watch what Owen did.

Owen looked at Sam's work and saw that he hadn't even started.

He thought to himself, "Sam must be having trouble with this. I'll help him," and he did.

Soon everyone, including Sam, had finished and the class was able to play a game.

Owen had helped Sam and the game was lots of fun.

Owen felt good.

Draw Jack at his math class

Draw Owen at his math class

Jack had been watching Owen closely but he still didn't know how he did it. No matter what happened Owen just seemed to make himself feel good about it and Jack just seemed to make himself feel bad about it.

Owen must have some kind of secret.

Jack wanted to know what he could do that would make him feel better.

Jack decided he would ask Owen to help him.

"Owen, how do you always know the best things to say and do, to make yourself feel good?" asked Jack.

"My body tells me," Owen told Jack.

"What do you mean?" said Jack.

"Well, when I start to feel bad, I know my body is telling me that I need to think or act differently," replied Owen.

"But how does your body tell you?" Jack wanted to know.

"By making me feel bad." Owen told Jack.

"But what do you mean? I don't understand." said Jack.

"O.K. When you feel bad, do you feel happy and relaxed or sad and angry?" Owen asked Jack.

"Um, sad and angry, I guess," answered Jack.

"When you feel bad does your stomach feel calm or do you have a sinking feeling in your stomach?" asked Owen.
"When I feel bad, I have a sinking feeling in my stomach," answered Jack.

"When you feel bad does your heart feel open or closed?" asked Owen.
"Closed, I guess," answered Jack.

"When you feel bad is it easy or hard for you to breathe?" asked Owen.
"It's hard to breathe," answered Jack.

"When you feel bad do you feel comfortable or uncomfortable in your own skin?" asked Owen.

"Very uncomfortable, like I want to run away from myself," answered Jack.

"Hey, I think I get it now," said Jack excitedly. "It's true; when I feel bad I feel angry and sad, I do have a sinking feeling in my stomach, my heart does feel closed, it is hard for me to breathe and I feel uncomfortable in my own skin."

"Well, that's how your body lets you know that whatever you just thought or did won't make you feel good," explained Owen.

"So, it's like your body is saying, 'No! Stop! Don't think like that! Don't do that!'" said Jack.

"Exactly", said Owen, "And, when you feel good, you feel happy and relaxed, your stomach feels calm, your heart feels open, it's easy for you to breathe and you feel comfortable in your own skin. That's how your body lets you know that whatever you just thought or did will make you feel good."

"So, it's like your body is saying, 'Yes! Go! Keep thinking like that! Keep doing what you just did!'" said Jack.

"That's exactly what your body is saying," Owen said

Jack was quiet for a minute, and then he looked at Owen with a worried look on his face. "What's wrong?" Owen asked.

"Well, I feel bad most of the time," Jack said in a worried voice.

"Oh, don't worry about that Jack. It just means that your body has been trying to get your attention for a while. You know Jack, lots of people think it's a bad thing when they feel bad," said Owen, "But, I don't. I think it's a good thing. As long as you understand what it means and you know what to do about it; you won't feel bad for long and you'll feel happier more of the time."

"O.K. Now I understand that when I feel bad it is my body's way of telling me that whatever I just thought or did won't make me feel good. But, how can I change the way I think or what I do?" asked Jack.

"Well, the first thing I do when I start to feel bad is say,
'Yahoo! I know what to do!'"

"What?" asked Jack with a puzzled look on his face.

'Let me explain,' said Owen.

"You know how I said it can be a good thing when you start to feel bad, as long as you understand what it means and what to do about it? Well, saying 'Yahoo!' reminds me that this is a good thing and that I'm about to do something to stop feeling bad and feel better."

"Also 'YAHOO also reminds me what I can do about it. You see YAHOO stands for **Y**ou **A**lways **H**ave **O**ther **O**ptions. (Options is another way of saying choices).

"So…" continued Owen, "'once you know that your body is telling you that you need to think or do something differently, you just say to yourself, **'What's another thought I could have about this?'** "
(That's another option or another choice)

"You think of at least two or three different thoughts you could have, you **tune in to your body**, and your body will let you know which thought will make you feel better." explained Owen.

"I also say a special rhyme that I made up to help me. It goes like this;
On or off?
Stop or go?
Does my body say yes?
Or does my body say no?"

"Can you give me an example?" asked Jack.

"Sure", said Owen. "You know the other day when we played basketball and we lost, my first thought was, "It was the umpires' fault! We should have won."

"That's what I thought too," interrupted Jack.

Owen went on, "But, then I started to feel bad, so I said to myself, **'Yahoo, I know what to do!' "**

Next I said, "What are some other thoughts I could have about this?"

One thought was, **"We would have won if I hadn't missed that three pointer".**
"I thought that thought, I tuned into my body, then I said the rhyme,

On or off?
Stop or go?
Does my body say yes?
Or does my body say no?"

"My body said, 'No'".

Another thought was, **"It doesn't really matter, it's only a game."**

"I thought that thought, I tuned into my body, then I said the rhyme,

On or off?

Stop or go?

Does my body say yes?

Or does my body say no?"

"My body didn't really say 'Yes' and it didn't really say 'No'. That's like my body telling me to keep going until I get a 'yes'."

My next thought was, **"Everyone played really well. It was a great game."**

"I thought that thought, I tuned in to my body, then I said the rhyme,

On or off?

Stop or go?

Does my body say yes?

Or does my body say no?"

"My body said, 'Yes'."

"So that's what I thought, and I felt good when I shook everyone's hand at the end of the game."

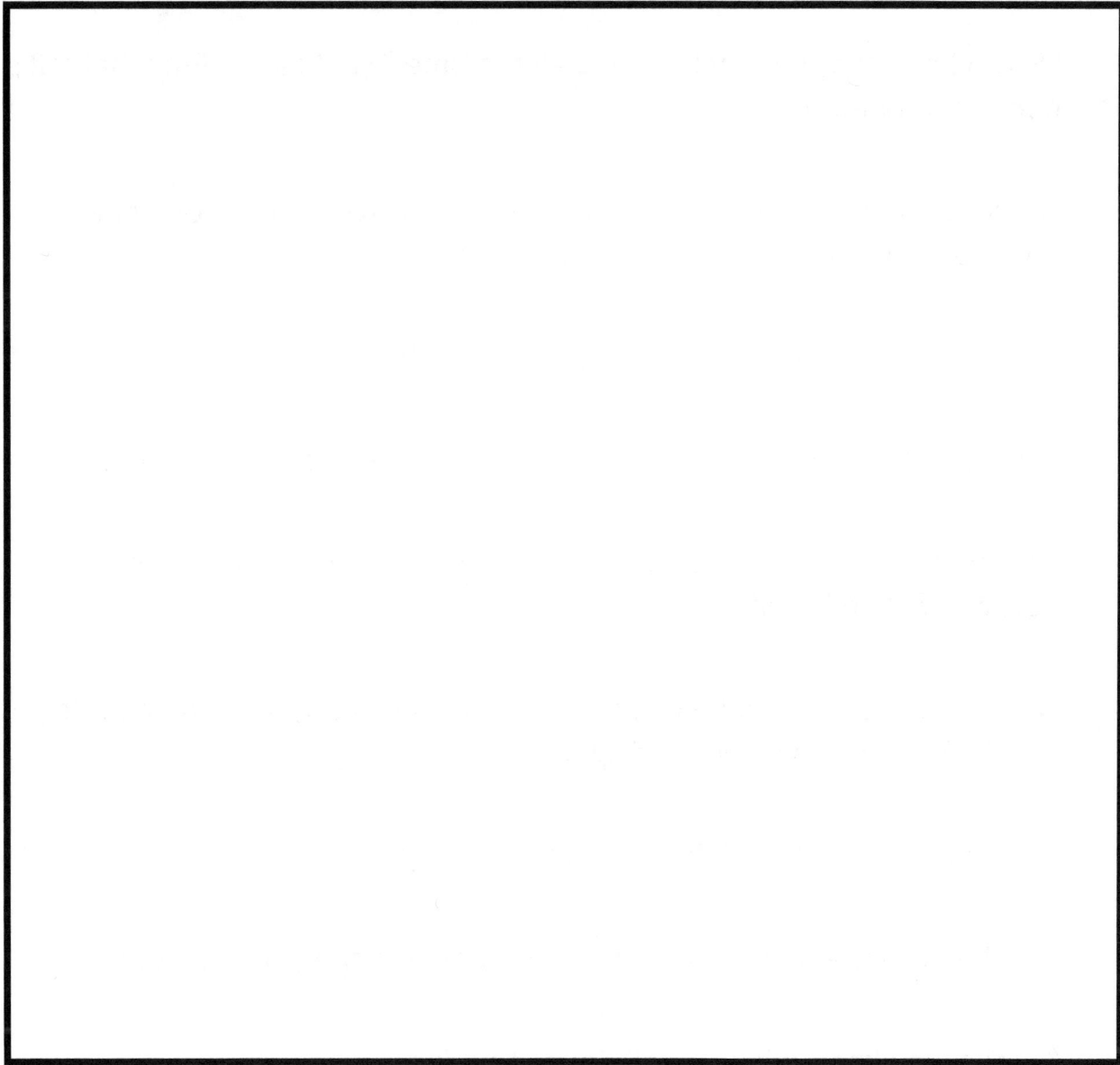

"Now I know why you feel so good all the time," said Jack. "But what if it doesn't work for me?"

"It works for everyone," Owen told Jack. "I'll prove it to you one day. Come on, let's go race our bikes in the park."

Owen and Jack lined their bikes up at the starting line.

"Ready, set, go!" shouted Jack, and off they went, racing along the track.

They were together all the way until just near the finish line Jack hit a pot hole and fell off his bike.

Owen stopped to see if he was O.K. He only had a tiny scratch on his leg. But, Jack looked angry and sad again.

"Hey Jack," Owen said, "What are you thinking?"

"I'm thinking that I never want to ride my bike ever again," sooked Jack.

"Yahoo, you know what to do!" Owen told Jack.

But Jack didn't answer, he was sulking.

"What's your body telling you Jack?" asked Owen.

"What do you mean what's my body telling me?" Jack shouted in an angry voice. "Gee Owen you're such a … ". Then Jack remembered what Owen had told him.

Jack tuned into his body.

"Well," said Jack, "I don't feel good, so I guess my body is telling me to think a different thought."

"Remember 'Yahoo! **Y**ou **A**lways **H**ave **O**ther **O**ptions'" Owen told Jack.

"So… what's another thought you could have about this Jack?" asked Owen.

"Um, I would have beaten Owen if I hadn't fallen off."
"What does your body say about that one, Jack?" asked Owen.

Jack tuned in to his body.

"Remember the rhyme." Owen reminded Jack.

"Oh yeah," said Jack.

"On or off?
Stop or go?
Does my body say yes?
Or does my body say no?"

"That wasn't really a yes or a no. So I keep going until I get a 'yes', is that right?"

"That's right. So, what's another thought you could have about this Jack?" asked Owen.

"Mmm, I know," Jack laughed, "I'll ask Owen to help me fill in that pot hole, race him again and beat the pants off him!"

"On or off?
Stop or go?
Does my body say yes?
Or does my body say no?"

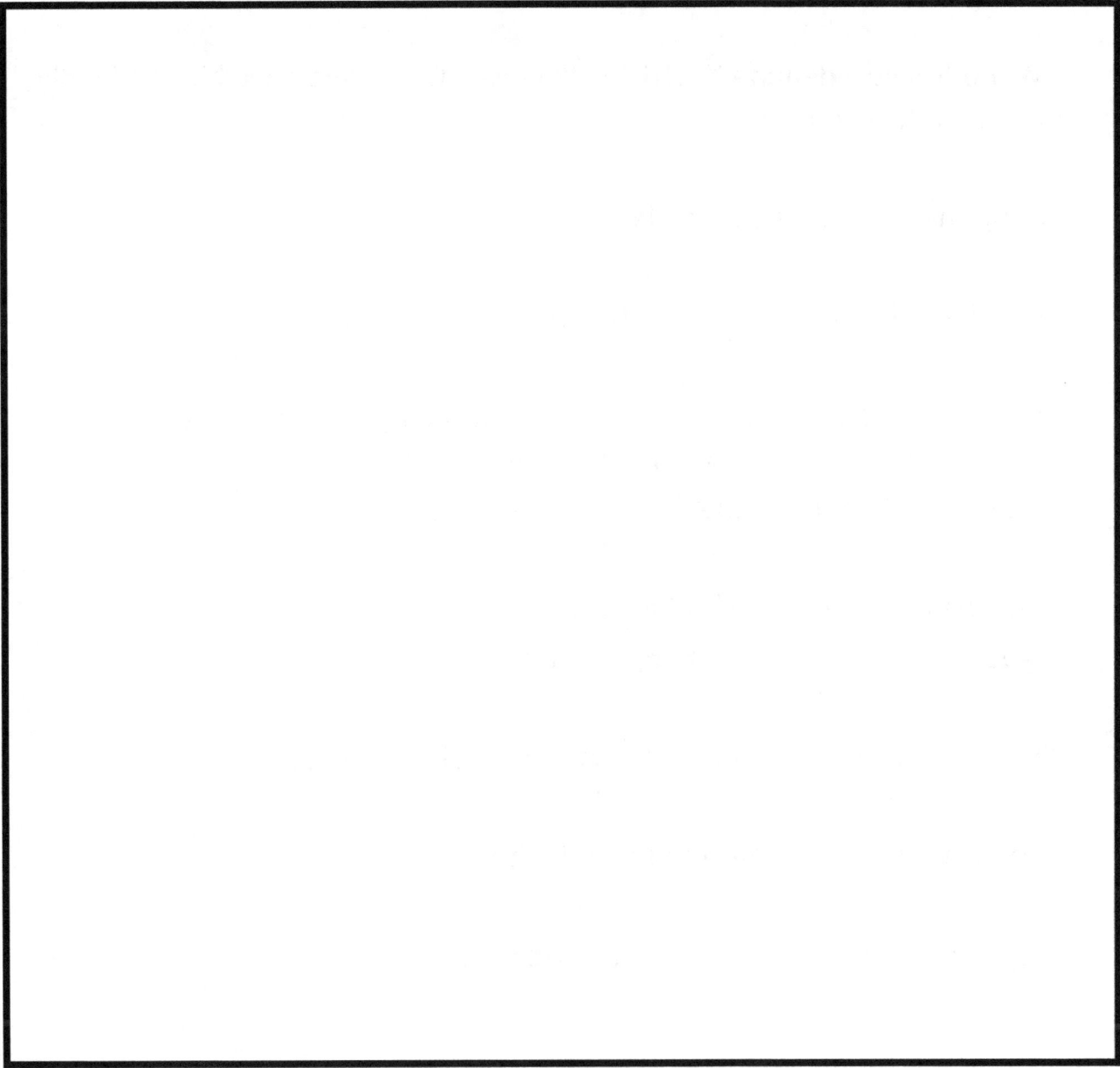

"My body said a definite YES!!!," Jack teased Owen and gave him a friendly punch on the shoulder.

"Good thinking, Jack!", Owen laughed.

"Hey, Jack, do you feel good on the inside?" asked Owen.

"No." Jack said, pretending to be angry and sad again. Then, with a big smile on his face, he threw his arms in the air and shouted,
"I feel GREAT on the inside!"

Owen had a big smile on his face too.
"I guess it worked for you then," he said.

"So that's the secret", Jack thought to himself, "how easy is that?"

But, he wanted to make sure he understood.

"So, let's just make sure I've got this right," said Jack.

"Whenever I feel bad, I say **'Yahoo!'** "

"Then, I **think of some different options** or choices,
I **tune into my body** and I say the rhyme for each one,
On or off?
Stop or go?
Does my body say yes?
Or does my body say no?"

"Then I just choose the one that feels the best."

"That's right." Owen told Jack.

"Wow! Thanks Owen." said Jack.

"Happy to help", replied Owen.

"Hey Owen, I've got a rhyme for you ..." said Jack.

"Yeah, what is it?" asked Owen.

Pointing to himself, Jack sang,

"Look at me smiling wide,
I'm feeling GREAT on the inside!"

I wonder if it will work for you too?

The next time you don't feel good on the inside...

Remember this is your body's way of telling you to think or do something different.

1. Say "**YAHOO**!
   I know what to do! "

2. Ask yourself
   "What's another thought I could have about this?"

3. Tune into your body
   Say the rhyme for each option

   " On or off?
   Stop or go?
   Does my body say yes?
   Or does my body say no? "

4. Choose the thought that feels the best

Information for Parents and Teachers

The **Yahoo series of 'Feel Good'** books are designed to work at the most fundamental level of how we are neurologically wired; the structure of the human brain.

The neural connections in our brain are formed by repetition and reinforcement. Learning to walk, talk, ride a bike, drive a car, read, write and so on are examples we can easily identify with to understand how we learn to do something.

The more we practise and reinforce any skills, the more automatic they become. When it becomes automatic for us, we no longer have to be conscious of what we're doing, we're just doing it.

Having a positive attitude and learning to feel good about ourselves can be understood in a similar way. As we repeat thoughts, emotions and actions over and over again, they become automatic patterns of behaviour; the way our brain is wired up.

What we may fail to understand is that the brain doesn't discriminate among thoughts on the neurological level. It takes no more effort to form a positive thought than it does a negative one. Attitudes are simply accumulations of related neural nets and positive attitudes are just as easy to construct as negative ones. (Evolve Your Brain By Joe Dispenza p.449).

Over time, by applying and practising the concepts presented in the 'Yahoo Feel Good' series of books this way of thinking will become the dominant/automatic way of thinking, feeling and acting because it's the way the brain has been wired.

It is recommended that your child illustrate the pages in this book. As your child is thinking about how to illustrate the concepts presented in the text, it will help stimulate and establish positive neural connections. Each time the story is re read or the concepts discussed, these connections will be activated and reinforced.

With consistent awareness, repetition and reinforcement, these thoughts will become beliefs; embedded in the child's neurology; the structure of their brain.

www.ingramcontent.com/pod-product-compliance
Lightning Source LLC
LaVergne TN
LVHW061341060426
835511LV00014B/2060

9780987317940